Super Mario Bros

Book 1

A Hilarious Super Mario Bros Adventure Story

Table of contents

Table of contents
Chapter 1 – Luigi In Trouble
Chapter 2 – A Brilliant Plan
Chapter 3 – Hoodwinking The Enemies
Chapter 4 – Into The Tunnels
Chapter 5 – A Daring Rescue
Chapter 6 – Luck Runs Out
Chapter 7 – A Terrible Mix Up
Chapter 8 – Dying Of Boredom
Chapter 9 – The Royal Schedule
Chapter 10 – Lost In Bowser's Fortress
Chapter 11 – A New Villain Appears
Chapter 12 – Unexpected Friends
Chapter 13 – An Inadvisable Nap
Chapter 14 – Princess Peach And The Tweester
Chapter 15 – Bowser And His Public Engagements
Chapter 16 – A Spooky House
Chapter 17 – A New Villain, Again
Chapter 18 – Diplomatic Relations
Chapter 19 – The Awful Truth
Chapter 20 – Where Is Mario?
Chapter 21 – Our Villains Meet

Chapter 22 - To The Rainbow Road

Chapter 23 - A Plan Is Formed

Chapter 24 - An Unusual Wedding

Chapter 25 - Bowser Doesn't Get It

Chapter 26 - Saving The Day

Chapter 27 - All's Well

Chapter 28 - Or Is It?

Copyright 2016 – All rights reserved.

Chapter 1 – Luigi In Trouble

Well, this wasn't supposed to happen.

Luigi jumped up and held onto the bars that covered the window. If he hung on, he could just see outside into the Mushroom Kingdom. In the distance, there were the green rolling hills and the happy citizens of the Kingdom, going about their day. Closer to him was a different story. Goombas, Koopas, and other various evildoers marched about, guarding the castle and looking generally menacing. Banners had been put up featuring Bowser's ugly mug. He couldn't see him out in the building's grounds, but he could imagine him sitting smugly in the throne room, where he didn't belong.

Ugh!

Luigi let go of the bars before his arms got tired. They'd been put in recently, but they were stuck solidly. He knew, he'd tried pulling them out all night and got nowhere. Well, a Koopa had seen what he was doing, looked in at him, then snorted and walked away. He knew he didn't have to watch Luigi very hard.

He sighed, and slumped down on the bed. There were worse prison cells, sure. There were soft furnishings everywhere, a bookcase packed full of romance novels and old journals, and the staff that weren't minions of Bowser seemed rather sorry for him. Every day they came by with delicious cakes and treats to keep his spirits up.

However, every time they came he could sniggering from the other side of the door. When he came to the hatch at the bottom of the door to collect his food it would stop, but as soon as it flapped shut again they'd walk down the hallway, openly laughing at him.

He plucked at the dress he was wearing and sighed again. If only he'd had his own clothes back! He wished he'd never thought of this stupid plan.

Chapter 2 – A Brilliant Plan

Three days earlier…

Mario and Luigi,

Please help! Bowser has taken control of my castle! He's locked me up in my quarters and he won't let me out! There's horrible creatures all over the place and they're scaring all the Toads.

I sent this letter with a Toad in the hope it'll find you. Please, you're the only two who can beat Bowser at his own game. Come kick him out and I can reward you both! I think we still have some cake left in the kitchens…

Love

Princess Peach xxx

Mario read the letter and shook his head.

'Again?' he said, gesturing to the letter in his hand. 'She's got to get better security.'

'I don't know, I heard the Toads are pretty tough' said Luigi.

'Not tough enough, they keep getting squished by Goombas.' Mario looked at the letter again. 'He's got her in her own place this time. What are we going to do? Bowser's fortress I can break into with my eyes closed and my hands tied behind my back.'

'How would you do that?'

'Run up to the door and kick it down, easy. Peach's castle, though... If he's brought his army there, they're going to be really careful who they let in.'

The pair sat in silence for a moment, thinking.

'If they see it's us, they're going to stop us in our tracks' Mario mused.

'That's why we go in disguise!' Luigi jumped out of his seat. 'Of course! We go as someone they're going to let inside!'

'That's brilliant! But who do we disguise ourselves as? I don't think either of us will pass for a Koopaling. Maybe we can build a giant Bullet Bill and have ourselves delivered to them?'

Luigi stared at him. 'No, that's ridiculous!'

Mario nodded. 'You don't get Bullet Bills delivered, they just show up and ruin the scenery.'

'I have an idea' said Luigi, 'But I'm going to need a few things.'

* * *

A few hours later...

Luigi came out of the dressing room grudgingly. Mario got one look at him, and rolled around laughing.

'I don't know what's so funny' Luigi grumbled. 'You should be wearing this.'

Mario stopped laughing for a moment and wiped the tears of laughter from his eyes. 'Oh no, it looks perfect on you. Besides, you're the same height. If I wore it, they'd know it was me. You'll get away with it.'

Luigi, still scowling, turned and looked in the mirror. He was wearing a bright blond wig, that curled it's way past his shoulders. A dainty gold tiara sat on top of the wig, that matched with the pretty pink parasol he was holding. What really set the outfit off, though, was the frilly pink dress he was wearing.

He had to admit, from a distance, he could be mistaken for Princess Peach. He turned around, trying to get a look at himself from all angles. Yes, pretty convincing, he thought.

'Well... it all looks OK. No one's going to be convinced when I get close up, though' he said.

'It doesn't matter by then. The plan is perfect. You wander in front of the castle gates, looking like you've just broken out. The guards will freak out, run to re capture you, and I'll run in with them while they're busy with you. Then, we can work on kicking them all out back to where they belong.'

Luigi shrugged. 'Just kick them out quickly, ok? I don't want to wear this any longer than I need to.'

'It'll be fine! It's your plan, aren't you sure about it?'

'When I made the plan, I thought it'd be you who'd be wearing the dress.'

Chapter 3 – Hoodwinking The Enemies

A few hours after that...

Mario and Luigi hid in the bushes outside Princess Peach's front doors. It was a sad sight. The pretty lakes and rivers surrounding the building had all dried up, leaving cracked, dry riverbeds in their wake. The sky above the castle had turned an ominous grey from all the smoke pouring from inside the walls. No doubt Bowser's minions were up to some evil deeds inside. The worst thing though was Bowser's minions themselves, walking around the castle as if they owned it. The very sight of it made them both suddenly sure that they were doing the right thing.

'Ok, you ready?'

Luigi adjusted his underskirts. 'As I'll ever be.'

He stepped out from behind the bushes, and wandered in front of the gates. At first, nobody spotted him. He looked at Mario, who was watching him between the branches.

'Get their attention!' he hissed.

'Er...' Luigi looked around him. What to do?

'Er... Oh no! What am I going to do?' he called in a high pitched voice. Mario looked at him oddly. Luigi shrugged.

'I'm out of the castle and I'm all on my own! Whatever will I do?'

A few of the Koopas patrolling turned round and looked at him.

'That's right... I'm all alone... no one to help me...' He was stood right out in the open. Why weren't they doing anything?

The Koopas looked at each other. Luigi panicked. Had they seen through the ruse? Did they know that he wasn't really Princess Peach? He wished they had a backup plan, but there wasn't one. If this didn't work, he was in serious trouble.

From the bush, Mario looked worried, too. Had he put Luigi in danger?

The Koopas had a low and hurried conversation with each other. Every now and then, one would op their head up and look at Luigi again. He turned to Mario.

'What are they doing?' he whispered.

'I don't know! You've got to get them to capture you before they get too suspicious!' he whispered back.

Luigi looked back. They were still whispering hurriedly. They must be deciding what to do with him. Quick, do something, anything!

'I... I think I'll just go over here... away from the doors' he called out in the same high pitched voice, loud enough for the bundle of Koopas to hear him. 'Away from all the guards, where no one will be able to catch me...'

The Koopas looked up at once. Luigi moved a step to the right, as if he was going to move away.

The lead Koopa yelled something, and pointed at Luigi. Then they all charged at once.

'Argh!' before he knew what was happening, Luigi was picked up and swept away on a sea of Koopas. From the corner of his eye, he could see Mario leap out of the bushes and sprint towards the crowd now carrying him through the castle doors. He squeaked through, just as they shut again.

It was dark inside, so he didn't see what happened next. He felt the group carry him up flight after flight of stairs. Everywhere was lit with gloomy torches, so he couldn't get his bearings. He had no idea where Mario had gone, but he knew the place maybe just as well as Princess Peach did. Maybe he'd found a secret passageway or a shortcut. He could only hope that was the case.

Just as he thought they couldn't get any higher up, he felt the group stop in the middle of a hallway. A door creaked open in the darkness, and he was unceremoniously tossed onto the floor. He heard the door slam shut, and the group walk away, muttering.

'Who's there?' came a voice.

Chapter 4 – Into The Tunnels

Mario sprinted through passageway after passageway, trying to keep away from Bowser's minions. Princess Peach's castle, like all castles, was a maze of secret hallways like these. He'd been here so often that he knew them like the back of his hand. Well, glove.

Just as he thought he could come out, another minion could be heard scurrying around outside, so he'd have to duck back in again. He carried on running, mapping the tunnels out in his head and deciding what to do next.

Not again. Princess Peach was always getting kidnapped. He thought Bowser did it at this point just to annoy him. He'd have to travel through all the lands, defeating all the monsters and raising all the flags, looking for the castle she'd been captured in. it always took a few goes, as she was always in another castle. ALWAYS.

He knew where he was going in Peach's home, but getting there would be another matter...

* * *

'Luigi, is that you?' The voice moved across the room and he could hear a match being struck. A flame flickered, then came to life in a lantern. Held above the head of the speaker, he could see that it was Princess Peach herself. 'It is! What are you doing in my bedroom?'

'Bedroom?' Luigi looked around him. Is that where he'd been taken?

'And... what are you *wearing*?'

Oh no. He'd forgotten about the dress and the wig.

'Er, um, Princess, I can explain...'

She giggled unexpectedly. 'Oh, I'd love to hear the story behind this.'

* * *

Two corridors and three turns back, Mario was sure he was on the right track. He ran as quickly as he could, not wanting to waste any time. They had Luigi, and who knew what they'd do to him when they found out who he was? Like Mario himself, he'd given them a lot of trouble in the past.

He slowed down on the next corner, and listened close to the wall. He could hear something big stomping about, barking orders at people. He thought about bursting in, taking them by surprise, but something made him lean in closer and listen to what was being said.

'GRAAAAAH! What do you mean she escaped?'

'She was outside the doors, Your Horribleness! We don't know how she got out! She's back now, though. Safe and sound. We have her under lock and key.'

'You said that the first time, and look what happened! How could she have got out? I put bars on her window and the doors locked shut! I want a guard on that door night and day!'

'Yes sir, right away sir!' The owner of the other voice scurried away, glad to get away from that horrible temper.

Bowser. Hard to be. No one else was as short tempered and angry as he was.

Mario thought about what the minion had said. The 'Princess Peach' they found had been locked away back in her cell, they'd said. If that was the case, they may have thrown Luigi in with the real Peach herself! If he could get there, he could bust them both out at once.

Now, where would Bowser have locked Peach up?

He knew it! Mario started running again.

Chapter 5 – A Daring Rescue

Luigi explained the whole plan, while Princess Peach listened intently. When he had finished, she sat back and looked at him.

'You know, it worked really well, didn't it?'

'Huh?' He looked at her blankly.

'Well, you got inside the castle. No one's been able to get in since Bowser took over. He's been really careful about that. I've been watching from the window. The minions have stopped anyone getting close.'

'Really?'

'Yes! Plus, now you're here, Mario will know where to find us both!'

'How?'

'Mario is smart, Luigi. He always finds me. He's so good at that.' She sat back and settled in. 'All we have to do is wait, now. He'll be here before we know it.

Luigi couldn't argue, but grumbled to himself a bit as they waited in the near darkness. It was always Mario, wasn't it? He was always the one to save the day. He got all the credit, and Luigi just had to sit on the sidelines and take it. Hadn't this whole thing been his idea? Would Mario have even got in without him? He didn't think so.

They sat in silence as they waited. Luigi didn't know what else to say to the princess. Why hadn't he realised they'd just lock her up in her bedroom? This was one of the strangest experiences of his whole life.

After a while, they began to hear rumblings, seemingly coming from the within the walls themselves. Luigi looked up. 'What's that?' he asked.

'It's Mario!' Princess Peach leapt up, clasping her hands together and smiling. 'He's come for us! You'll see! I said he would!'

Peach danced up and down, clapping her hands. 'I knew it!' she cried.

'Shh! The guards might hear you!'

Peach sat down, slightly crestfallen. 'Oh, ok.'

The rumbling grew louder.

'What's he doing?' Luigi whispered.

'He's found the right passageway, he's making his way up here' Peach replied. 'He won't be long now.'

A few minutes later, the noise grew even louder, accompanied by the screeching of what sounded like heavy machinery.

'Is that a dr-' Luigi started to say. He couldn't finish, because at that moment Mario burst through the wall, riding what appeared to be a giant drill. It screeched to a halt halfway across the room.

'Haha!' Mario called out. 'It's me!'

'Mario!' Peach jumped up again, flung her arms around him, and kissed him on the cheek. 'I knew you'd come.'

'Well, it was Luigi's plan, but yes, I'm here now!' He turned and grinned at Luigi. 'See! I knew it would all turn out ok!'

'We've got to kick Bowser out yet' Luigi responded, darkly.

'Yes, and I'll need your help. Come on, you two, let's get you out of here. We'll go to the throne room and take him out!' he cried. 'Follow me!'

Chapter 6 – Luck Runs Out

The three heroes made their way back down the secret passageway that had led to Princess Peach's bedroom and makeshift cell. They had to kick rubble out of the way where Mario had drilled his way up there. It seemed that this passageway hadn't been used in a long time. There were plenty of rocks and rubble where the walls had caved in, and spider webs adorned the ceiling.

Princess Peach picked her way daintily through all the mess. Mario and Luigi just ran straight through, not minding that they were getting covered in dust and dirt.

Before long, there was a light at the end of the passage. Mario slowed down, but hadn't warned Luigi, who bumped right into the back of him. They both fell over and splayed out on the grimy floor.

'Argh!' Luigi yelled. 'Warn us next time you do that!'

Mario picked himself up, and held his hand out for his brother. Luigi took it and was hauled back up onto his feet.

'Here we are' he whispered. 'This will take us straight to the throne room.'

'Ugh, I bet he's ruined it' said Peach.

'Probably, buy we can worry about that later.' Mario gestured for them to follow him. 'Be quiet, and don't say a thing unless I say so.'

They followed him in silence as the light grew brighter. Soon, they could see they were entering the throne room from behind the throne itself.

'It's not ready yet! WHY ISN'T IT READY? GRAAAAAH!' They could hear stomping and smashing happening in front of the throne. 'This needs be done now! Yesterday! As soon as possible!'

'Yes, sir I know...' said a minion, meekly.

'We have to get it done NOW! Any minute now, that meddling plumber will show up and start trying to ruin everything!'

'I think that's our cue' said Mario under his breath. He opened the door that lead out into the throne room proper, and stepped out around Peach's throne, now broken and smudged in who knew what.

'You called?' he asked.

Bowser turned round and growled. 'How did you get in here?'

'That's none of your business. And I think it's time for you to leave' said Mario, defiantly. 'You have your own fortress. Why do you need Princess Peach's, too?'

'Because I need Princess Peach' said Bowser.

'What for?'

'Never you mind! Guards? Get him!'

The minions came running, but Mario was ready for them. He climbed up on the throne and jumped off, making his way across the throne room by jumping on Goomas' heads.

Boing, boing, boing... as he went, more minions went running for cover, and Bowser roared his disapproval.

'GET BACK HERE! FIGHT HIM, YOU COWARDS!'

As Mario bounced his way around defeating the minions, Luigi and Princess Peach made their way out to see what was going on.

'My throne room!' Princess Peach cried, dismayed. It was easy to see why. Bowser had only been here a couple of days, but he'd made his mark on it. The room as Luigi remembered it was always pristine, every surface gleaming as hardworking Toads did their best to keep it looking beautiful.

Under Bowser's command, things were a different story. Every surface was covered in muck, dirt, or something unspeakable. It looked as though someone had been driving go karts around in here, leaving track marks all over the floor. The carpets were all torn, and the walls were scuffed and dirty. Princess Peach looked as though she were about to cry.

'Look what he did to my throne!' she wailed.

At that, Bowser turned round. Mario stopped bouncing, and the remaining minions ran while they still could.

'Princess Peach?' Bowser growled. 'But... there's two of you?'

'She's out of her cell, you can't hold her anymore! Get out while you still can!' called Mario, from the other side of the room.

'I don't think so. You thought you could fool me, huh? You trying to make a fool of me?'

'No one's trying' Luigi muttered under his breath. Peach nudged him.

'Don't be rude' she said.

Bowser came towards them threateningly. Luigi's knees knocked together, but he tried not to how scared he was.

'Try to confuse me with two Peaches? You think I'm stupid? HAH!' he yelled. 'I know which ones the real Peach! Bad luck, Mario!'

He leaned down and swept up a Peach in one giant paw.

'And now, you two are going far away' he roared. He picked up the other Peach and Mario in the other paw, then stomped over to the window. 'You'll never find your way back now!'

With that, he leaned back, and flung the two of them as far as he could throw them.

Chapter 7 – A Terrible Mix Up

'Aaaaargh!'

They flew what felt like forever through the air, the Mushroom Kingdom speeding past below them. Where were they going to land?

The answer came soon enough.

The land started rushing up to greet them, and before either of them had a chance to scream, they found themselves crashing through a roof and landing with a thud on a cold, flagstone floor.

Mario stood up and brushed himself off.

'Well, what's plan B?' he asked, reaching out to help his brother up.

The figure in the dress rolled over and groaned.

'Princess Peach?'

She nodded, and stood up. 'That's me.'

'But if you're here, then Luigi...'

Realisation dawned on Peach's face.

'Bowser has him, thinking he's me!'

'Oh no, what have I done?'

* * *

Bowser pounded back up the stairs, Luigi still gripped tight in one meaty claw. He opened the door to Peach's room and flung him inside.

'There, Princess. Now stop playing these silly games. Soon you'll be all mine, so you shouldn't fight it.'

'But I'm not - '

'Oh, I know you don't like it, but it'll all be for the best. Don't you want to live with me, Princess? Don't you think it would be wonderful? Our kingdoms, united at last! We'd have to throw the Toads out though. Too untidy. Mushroom Kingdom would look much better inhabited by my citizens, don't you think?'

'But I'm not -'

'Stop ARGUING, princess! You'll do as I say and that's the end of it! Now, I've got some very important things to do. You sit tight, it'll only be a couple of days and this will all be over.'

Bowser stomped off back down the corridor, leaving Luigi to his own thoughts.

Well, now what?

Mario and Princess Peach were who knew where. Bowser had thrown them so far they'd disappeared over the horizon. He didn't doubt that once he realised what had happened, Mario would come back for him. However, what was he going to do in the mean time?

He looked around him. There was nothing in here that could aid his escape. After all, it was just Peach's bedroom. He saw that the entrance to the secret passageway had been bricked over already by an industrious minion, so he couldn't even get out that way.

He walked over to the wardrobe and looked inside. As expected, it was full of dresses. He couldn't even get changed out of this stupid dress.

He flopped down on the bed. He was in for a long wait...

Chapter 8 – Dying Of Boredom

Mario and Princess Peach looked around them.

'Where are we?' Peach asked.

Mario took in the lakes of lava that spat fire all around them, and the raised walkways within the dark stone building. 'I think this is Bowser's castle' he said.

Peach looked shocked. 'But we're so far away! We have to get back, Mario! He still has Luigi! What will he do when he finds out he isn't me?'

Mario was thinking the same thing. This was all his fault. He should have defeated Bowser more quickly. If he had, everyone would be safe by now.

Out loud, he said 'We need to get going, then. The sooner we get back to the castle, the sooner we can save Luigi.'

'Right.' Princess Peach nodded. 'Lead the way.'

'Don't you know the way out by now, Peach? You've been here often enough.'

She visibly bristled at that. 'Yes, when I was captured. I only saw the inside of a cell, Mario.'

Mario took her hand and began leading her away down the walkways. 'Sorry. Let's get going in any case.'

'That's ok.' Peach allowed herself to be lead.

They walked for what felt like hours through the passageways and walkways of the building. Bowser had been serious about creating a fortress when he built his home.

'Do you know where you're going?' Peach asked, as they hit another dead end.

'I thought I did' Mario grumbled. They turned around to head back and find another way to go, but there was something stopping them in their tracks.

It looked like a Koopa, but scarier, if you could believe that. It was no longer turtle like in appearance, as it had been reduced down to its very skeleton. It looked at them with its eyeless sockets, and rattled its bones in a threatening manner.

'A Dry Bones!' Peach shrieked. She dove behind Mario and cried, 'Stop it!'

Mario stared it down. A Dry Bones was no match for him, even when he was taken by surprise.

They stared at each other for a moment. Without warning, the Dry Bones darted forward. As if he had been waiting for it, Mario jumped up and off the wall to his right, leaping onto the creature from above. He landed squarely on its head, driving it into the ground and reducing its bones to dust.

Princess Peach remained cowering in the corner. 'Is it gone?'

'It's gone!' Mario went to her and put his hand out, which Peach took gratefully. She got back up and looked around cautiously. 'Will there be more?'

'I can almost guarantee it' he said. Peach gulped.

'You'll protect me though, won't you Mario?'

Mario nodded. 'Like I always do.'

* * *

Luigi kicked his heels against the bed, chin in his hands. It had been only a few hours, and he was bored already. How long were Mario and Princess Peach going to be? Days, probably. Days and days of waiting, locked in Peach's tower bedroom. How was he going to pass the time?

He looked around him. Peach had been locked in here before him. She must have been doing something before they both showed up. How had she been keeping herself entertained?

There was a bookcase filled with books in one corner. He wandered over and pulled a few out at random. They were mostly romance novels with pictures of doe eyed lovers on the cover. He read the titles out loud with increasing disgust.

I Fell In Love With A Koopa.

It's Me Or The Goomba.

Teaching The Blooper How To Love.

He threw them over his shoulder as he read the titles out. These were all awful! He couldn't read these! It'd be worse than the time he tried to read Mario's plumber's manual when they'd run out of books to read at home. Who read romance novels? Yawn.

He flopped back onto the bed. He'd either have to work out how to escape, or die of boredom.

Chapter 9 – The Royal Schedule

Bowser stomped around the throne room, angrily. A timid Koopa stood in the corner, scribbling notes onto a scroll and Bowser ranted and raved.

'Bring it forward! We need to get everything done before the princess decides to run for it again' he said, sulking. 'She doesn't know what's good for her' he added under his breath. The Koopa heard him, but chose wisely to pretend he hadn't.

'How soon, Your Horribleness?' he asked.

'As soon as you can! You know what she's like. Any sign of trouble and she starts yelling for those idiot plumbers to come help her. They're a nightmare! A nuisance! They're pests! They're everywhere! GRAAAAH!' He picked up a chair and smashed it against the opposite wall. The Koopa flinched.

'We can do it in three days' said the Koopa, checking his notes.

'Three days? THREE DAYS? She'll be gone by then! Why can't we have it sooner?'

'Well, Your Horribleness, we can't have it tomorrow as you have to go stomp the neighbouring kingdoms to stop them coming and fighting you.'

'Right. Got to show them who's boss, smash a few houses, make them scared.'

'Yes. The day after, you've got to make a tour of the Mushroom Kingdom.'

'Why?'

'Because the inhabitants need to know that you'll be their ruler soon. You've got to show your face, kiss a few babies, that kind of thing.'

'Kiss babies? You've got to be kidding.'

'No one will be happy with you staying if you eat them rather than kiss them. Once the princess problem has been solved, you can do what you like. The day after that, you have a spa day planned, remember.'

'Oh, yes.'

'We can cancel that if you like and bring it up a day?'

'No! No. That day took ages to schedule in. I'm not losing the booking now.'

'Ok, that settles it. I'll book it in three days from now.'

'Fine. You may go.'

The Koopa scuttled away, glad to be out of Bowser's sight. Bowser lowered himself down into the already dilapidated throne. It groaned and splintered under his giant weight, and more small parts broke off and flew away. The throne room was getting messier by the hour.

He sighed. That uppity princess. She'd learn her place, sooner rather than later. If only she knew how happy she'd be with him ...

Chapter 10 – Lost In Bowser's Fortress

Mario and Princess Peach continued through Bowser's fortress, still looking for the exit.

Mario was tired and wanted to give up. Were the walls changing behind him? He felt like he was walking in circles. Princess Peach was flagging behind him, but she wouldn't complain. He knew she wouldn't say anything even if her feet fell off. She'd be too polite to say anything.

He wondered what they were going to do. How were they ever going to get back to Luigi and save the Mushroom Kingdom.

After a while of gloomy silence as he worried about these things, Princess Peach perked up and pointed ahead of them. 'Who are they?' she whispered to him.

He looked up. In the distance, there was a gang of people blocking their only way forward. He held out an arm to stop Peach, and they both stood there and considered their options.

'I can't see who they are from here' he said, 'but I'm pretty sure they're not friendly.'

'Brr, I hope it's not more of those skeletons' said Peach.

Mario chose not to tell her that Dry Bones would reanimate themselves from time to time.

'We can't go any further forward without running into them' he said. 'I don't think I can fight them all at once.'

Peach thought for a moment. 'Maybe we don't have to fight them.'

Mario turned and stared at her. 'What? They're the bad guys Princess, they don't listen to you, they just knock you into pits, or jump on you, or...' he trailed off, looking at her horrified expression.

'Is that what they do?'

'Well, if they're feeling... unfriendly' he said, lamely.

Princess Peach pulled herself up to her full height. 'Well, we'll see about that' she muttered, and began marching towards the shadowy figures.

'Peach, wait!' Mario hissed at her, as he ran to catch up. 'What are you doing?'

'What I do best' she said, not looking at him. As they drew closer, he could see that the gang of bad guys were actually Magikoopas. They waved their wands threateningly as they got closer.

'Princess, this is a bad idea, they're dangerous, let me handle them' he pleaded, but she didn't even acknowledge him. She marched right up to the group, and then held out her hand. 'I'm Princess Peach, ruler of the Mushroom Kingdom' she announced. 'I'm very pleased to meet you.'

The Magikoopas just stared at her. Peach continued holding out her hand, waiting for a response.

'Good afternoon, gentlemen. Or is it good morning? Or good night? Do you know, I can't tell in this place.'

They continued to stare at her. Peach started looking worried.

'I'm sorry, do you understand me?' She turned to Mario. 'Maybe we don't speak the same language, I never thought -'

'We understand you, Princess.' One Magikoopa stepped forward, the hood of his cloak covering his eyes. 'We understand you just fine.'

Peach's face broke out into a huge smile. 'Oh, that's wonderful!' she declared. 'I say, my friend and I have found ourselves lost here, and we were hoping of you could escort us out of the fortress? We don't want to be a bother.'

'Oh ,we can escort you, all right.' The Magikoopa began to snigger, which set off a chain reaction of snickers in the rest of the group.

'Mario? Why are they laughing?' she whispered.

'Because they're nasty pieces of work.' Mario sighed. This wasn't going to end well.

The lead Magikoopa lifted his wand. 'I'll escort you, *princess*. We know where you need to go!'

He waved the wand, and -

Chapter 11 – A New Villain Appears

'Urrrgggh.'

Mario rolled over and looked up into a sea of stars. Next to him, Princess Peach stirred.

'Where are we now?' she mumbled into the stone floor.

'I have no idea.' He picked himself up, and she did the same. What had the Magikoopas done?

The room was huge and round, the ceiling open to the night sky. The walls rose for what felt like miles into the black sky. They were stood on a stone platform in the middle of a lake of pure lava. Sparks jumped and sizzled as they watched. There was no way off, as far as Mario could see. They were stuck.

'We're in trouble, aren't we?' Peach asked, looking around in vain for a way out.

'Not yet' he said, although privately he thought they were doomed.

Just as they thought they were done for, they heard a familiar voice come from the darkness.

'HahaHA! Look what we have here! It's the Mushroom Kingdom's favourite loser, and his damsel in distress!'

They heard a flapping noise, and then the strangest flying machine they'd ever seen flapped over the dungeon's walls. It appeared to be some kind of bicycle, held aloft by huge flapping birds wings. They felt the hot air of the dungeon pushed into their faces as it came closer towards them. Sitting atop the machine was none other than -

'Wario?' Mario cried out.

'You scoundrel!' Peach shook her fist. 'Did you do this?'

'You bet I did!' Wario brought his flying machine to a stop in mid air, the huge wings flapping to keep it aloft. The wind pushed Mario and Peach's hair back. 'Things were getting boring, don't you think? Now you have a challenge! How are you getting out of here? What say you, Mario?'

Mario glared at him.

'Nothing to say? That's unusual for such a big hero like you. What, aren't you going to save the day?'

'What do you want, Wario?' he asked.

'What do I want? Well, it's very simple. I want you to entertain me!' He cackled again. 'You're doing a great job so far! Dressing Luigi up as the Princess! Getting him kidnapped! Ending up here! Ho ho, you're doing an excellent job!' He leaned back and howled with laughter. 'You're hilarious!'

Princess Peach clenched her fists. 'You think this is funny?' she snarled. Mario was taken aback. In all his time knowing her, he'd never seen her so angry.

'I don't think this is funny, I think this is HYSTERICAL!' Wario howled with laughter again. 'Oh, I'm so glad I convinced that idiot lizard to take over your castle! Why hadn't he thought of it before? Oh, I want to see his dumb scaly face when he finds out Luigi isn't you!' He wiped tears from his eyes. 'Oh, this is wonderful!'

'You put Bowser up to it?' Princess Peach seethed.

'Of course I did!'

'And you put everyone in the Mushroom Kingdom in danger?'

'Oh come on Princess, this is just a bit of fun. Don't you see how funny it is?'

'And it's your fault that that horrible monster is in MY castle?'

As Mario watched, steam began to pour out of Peach's ears. Her face turned bright red, and she began to tremble.

'You'll be sorry!' she yelled at Wario. 'You won't think this is funny when it's all over!'

Wario started to laugh at her, but stopped abruptly. Peach had caught on fire. He could barely see her through the flames, but she was still stood rigid, staring with an intense fury at Wario.

'I've heard ENOUGH. We're going back to my home, Mario. Come on!' She reached out and grabbed him. Without warning, she jumped up into the sky, and flew straight over the dungeon walls. Mario could just hear Wario's confused 'Whaaaaa?' before they disappeared over the other side.

Chapter 12 – Unexpected Friends

They landed with an almighty thud outside Bowser's fortress. As they came steaming towards the ground, Mario could see minions running for cover, screaming. When they landed, the ground actually shook. Mario stumbled away, his head spinning. He nearly toppled over, but he grabbed hold of a rotten old stone wall at the last minute.

'Princess, what was that?' he stammered.

She shrugged. 'I was angry. It was rather unbecoming, I should control my temper next time. But he made me so angry!' She threw her neatly gloved hands up into the air. 'What else was I supposed to do?'

'Princess, how long have you been able to do that?'

'Ever since I can remember.'

She seemed so unworried about the entire thing. Was this why she never got angry?

'That was incredible! You got us out of there! We'd have never escaped without you!' he declared. He was seeing Peach in an entirely new light.

'I suppose. I don't like to get angry very often.' Princess Peach brushed some dust from her skirt. 'What do we do now?'

Mario looked out into the desert which stretched away from them. 'We go rescue Luigi' he said.

*   *   *

The Blooper looked lovingly into my eyes.

'I know I'm a Toad and you're an underwater monster, but somehow, we can make this work!' I said to him. 'It's forbidden, but I know you're my one true love!'

The Blooper looked at me with his blank eyes, but I knew he was trying to express how he felt without words. How much he loved me. How much I meant to him. How he couldn't live without me.

He squirted ink into my face.

Luigi devoured page after page, revelling in how ridiculous the story was. He howled with laughter as he tore through the book. He couldn't believe that anyone took these stories seriously.

As he finished the book and started on *From The Dry Dry Desert, With Love,* he heard a knock at the door. It wasn't time for dinner. He shut the book and sat up, listening carefully.

'Psssst!'

What?

'Pssssssssssst!'

He padded over to the door. 'Who is it? he whispered.

'It's a friend' the voice answered. 'Take this note. Read it then burn it. Memorise it carefully.'

A piece of paper slid under the door, then there was the sound of footsteps retreating.

Luigi bent over and picked up the note. He unfolded it, and read the message contained within.

Dear Luigi,

We know it's you locked up in there, but don't worry, we won't tell. Bowser may be stupid enough not to notice, but we did. Sit tight, we'll get you out of there as soon as we can. We want to go home as much as you want us out of here.

Your friends.

xxx

Luigi looked up, puzzled. Who were his friends. Who knew he was here, apart from Mario and Princess Peach? He read the note several times, but he couldn't make head nor tail of it. In the end, he knew the note back to front. He did as the writers asked, and burned the note in the fireplace.

Who were his friends in the castle?

Chapter 13 – An Inadvisable Nap

Mario and Princess Peach trudged through the desert. They walked across mile upon mile of hot sand. Wind blew sand into their faces. Sand got into their shoes. Sand found its way into their clothes. Sand was everywhere.

Mario blew sand out of his moustache. 'This is ridiculous' he muttered.

They boiled under the blazing sun. Peach visibly wilted, dragging her skirts behind her as she walked along. Mario's hat looked like it was melting, the sides of it having fallen down. They were now flapping against his face as he walked.

Flap, flap, flap. Flap, flap, flap.

'How much further?' asked Peach, after they'd walked for what felt like hours.

'I don't know' he said. As he said it, he heard something *flop* onto the ground behind him. He turned around, to see Princess Peach had just dropped to the ground and was now lying spread out on the sand.

'It's so hot' she said, simply.

Mario stopped and sat down next to her. 'We have to keep going' he said weakly, but the call of the ground was just too irresistible.

'Maybe we can lie down for just a minute.' he said. 'Just to keep our strength up.'

They were both asleep within seconds.

* * *

Bowser stomped a house into the ground, and laughed as the family ran away, screaming,

'GWAHAHA! Don't mess with me, peasants!' He stomped his way over to another house, and had just raised his foot to stomp it into oblivion when his Koopa assistant called out to him.

'Your Horribleness?'

'WHAT? Can't you see I'm busy?'

The family who lived in the house stood nearby, cowering.

'I'm sorry, Your Horribleness, but it's important. Our contact at Bowser castle says that Mario escaped with an unknown partner.'

'WHAT?' Bowser put his foot down and walked over to the assistant. The family breathed a sigh of relief.

'He said they'd jumped over the wall and ran away' said the assistant, who was now trembling himself. No one liked having to give Bowser bad news. The last assistant he'd had had been thrown into the lava pits for giving Bowser a bowl of cake without his favourite ice cream. This Koopa had ended up with the job because he'd drawn the short straw.

'He jumped over the walls? How? No one can jump that high!' Bowser thought for a moment. 'Except me, of course.'

'Of course', the Koopa quickly agreed.

'Well, where did he go?' asked Bowser.

'The contact said that he wandered out into the Dry Dry Desert.'

'Oh, good. He won't last for five minutes out there. Look, am I done here? Only I want to get back to the castle. Cook said he was making fish heads for lunch.'

'We can be if you think you're done?' The Koopa looked at the family, who were still eyeing them warily.

'Yes, I should say so. I'm bored now. Why do almighty rulers have to do this sort of thing? It's beneath me.' Bowser started to walk away back to the castle.

'Of course, Your Horribleness.' The Koopa began to skitter after him. The family ran back into their home, and shook their fists at Bowser out of the window.

Chapter 14 – Princess Peach And The Tweester

Mario was awoken by something pulling at his clothes.

'Mrrrrfivemoreminutes' he mumbled into his sleeve.

The pulling grew harder.

'MrrrrrWHAT?'

His hat nearly blew off his head. Fully awake within a second, he grabbed the hat and pulled it firmly back down. He turned round to see Princess Peach floating in midair, pulling at her skirts to keep them down.

'What's happening?' she yelled out to him.

He looked at his feet and realised that he, too, was floating. He couldn't see anything past that, as they were encircled by flying sand. It scraped past his face as they rose, higher and higher into the air.

'Oh no!' he yelled back. 'It's a Tweester!'

A Tweester was a particularly nasty desert enemy. It would pick you up when you least expected it, and try and drag you off into new and unfamiliar territory. It would usually be dangerous, so desert explorers were always warned to be wary of them. How could he have let them both fall asleep?

'What are we going to do?' Peach called out to him.

'I don't know! Tweesters stop only when they want to stop!'

They carried on, the Tweester carrying them across the desert. After a while, Mario saw something he wished he hadn't. They were heading straight towards a huge cliff. It would surely throw them over the side. How would they ever get out?

'Noooo' he said to himself. Peach overheard.

'What is it?' she said, her face full of concern.

Mario couldn't lie to her. 'That cliff, we're going to go straight over it.'

'We can't! We'll never get out!'

'I think that's the idea.'

Princess Peach's face crumpled.

'What do you mean? We can't over it, we have to go save Luigi!'

Tears began to run down her cheeks.

'We can't let this happen! Poor Luigi will be stuck there forever! Who will save him if we're lost in this desert? It's so unfair!'

She began to sob, rivers flowing down her face now.

'I JUST WANTED TO SAVE LUIGI AND GET MY CASTLE BACK FROM THAT AWFUL BOWSER! HE'S RUINING IT! EVERYONE WILL BE SAD AND IT'S ALL MY FAULT!'

Mario was at a loss as to what to do.

'It'll be ok' he said, unsure of what would help. 'We'll get out and get to the castle, don't you worry.' It sounded weak even to his own ears.

'NO IT WON'T!' she wailed. 'I'VE RUINED EVERYTHING! THE TOADS WILL HATE ME!'

The tears from her eyes form gushing waterfalls, streaming from both sides of her face. They fell and fell, and it seemed like Peach would never stop crying. Mario was wondering how he was going to make her stop when he realised they were getting lower. The ground below them was wet with tears, and it was slowing the Tweester down!

Peach continued to howl and sob. The Tweester got slower and slower as the sand it was pulling up got wetter and wetter. Soon, they were nearly touching the ground. When he thought it was safe, he leaned over and grabbed Peach's arm. She stopped crying abruptly, and looked at Mario like she'd never seen him before. He yanked them both out of the now feeble Tweester, and they both fell to the ground and rolled a fair way before stopping.

Mario stood up and brushed sand out of his hat, wondering if he was ever going to make a soft landing on this trip. Princess Peach sat on the sand, honking delicately into a silk handkerchief.

'I'm sorry Mario, I don't know what came over me' she said. 'It was very unladylike.' She stood up, and began brushing sand out of her skirt.

'Princess, don't you see what you just did?' Mario exclaimed. 'You stopped a Tweester! All by yourself! No one's ever been able to do that before!'

'I did?' Peach looked around, and seemed astonished to see that they had escaped. 'So I did! Well, would you look at that!' She seemed rather bemused by the whole thing.

Mario wondered if Princess Peach was even more powerful than she appeared. He took her hand. 'Look, we're nearly out of the desert' he said. He gestured into the distance, where a forest was just starting to take shape. 'Look, we're nearly there. Let's go and get out of the sun.'

Princess Peach smiled her bright smile at him. 'Yes, let's.'

Chapter 15 – Bowser And His Public Engagements

Luigi was happily reading his way through *Chosen By My Boo* when another knock came on his door. He stood up and went over.

'Luigi, are you there?'

'Where else would I be, I'm locked in here!'

'Oh. Yes. Sorry.' The voice coughed. 'Look, we're trying very hard to get you out, but you might have to wait a little while longer.'

'Why?'

'Because we can't take you out safely with Bowser noticing you yet. Look, just sit tight, ok? We're trying our hardest to come up with a plan. Will you be ok until then?'

Luigi looked over to the pile of books he had waiting for him.

'Yeah, I'll be fine' he said.

* * *

Bowser trundled along in his car, waving to the inhabitants of the Mushroom Kingdom. Toad after Toad stared back at him, frowning. It was all rather odd when he'd asked for the music and confetti to lighten the mood.

'Why aren't they smiling?' he asked the Koopa assistant, as another batch of confetti was fired off, and rained down into more dark faces. 'Who doesn't love confetti? Or a marching band? It's a party, for crying out loud!'

'Because they're quite upset you have the Princess locked up' replied the assistant, who was sat next to him. 'They do really like her, you know.'

'Well, it's only for another day' said Bowser. 'You'd think they'd understand that.'

'They don't really take kindly to being locked up for any length of time' explained the Koopa. 'There's not much we can do about that.'

'Didn't you all explain it to them?'

'We did. Multiple times. They were very upset.'

'How do you know?'

'They slammed doors in our faces, shooed us away from their homes. One Koopa got the contents of a chamber pot dumped on his head.'

'Urgh.'

'Exactly.'

'Well, you'd think they'd cheer up, at least. Things will get better soon!' He waved at the nearby crowds, stretching his jaws into an unconvincing grin. A baby Toad began to cry.

'Well, I'm trying my best' he shrugged.

Chapter 16 – A Spooky House

Mario and Princess Peach had made it into the forest. They walked along delightful paths, full of sunshine coming down through the branches of the trees, and the wonderful scent of the flowers that grew in abundance. Peach walked along the path and animals flocked to her. Songbirds sat on her shoulders, deer nipped at her heels, and rabbits hopped along at her feet. It was as perfect and idyllic as it got in the forest.

As they moved further in, though, the animals began to peel away. As the last deer slunk away, Mario noticed the trees were growing in closer and closer together. Soon, there was almost no sunlight at all coming in through the branches. The few pin pricks of light that did make it through showed the ground becoming brown and dusty, the lush grass of the forest now just a distant memory. Somewhere in the distance, a wolf howled.

'Well, that was too good to last' Mario commented. Peach looked worried.

'It's just dark in here, right? We'll move further along and we'll reach the other edge of the forest, right?'

'Hopefully.' In truth, Mario just wasn't sure.

The further they walked, the gloomier it seemed to get. After a while of walking, Princess Peach said, 'can you see that? In the distance?'

Mario peered through the trees to where Peach was pointing. There was something there, it was true. He couldn't make out what it was, though. Whatever it was, this deep into the forest, it couldn't be good. They'd come this far though, and they couldn't turn back.

'We'll walk up and see what it is' he said, praying it wasn't anything that would try and eat them, or stop them in their quest. Or tell annoying riddles. Mario hated riddles.

As they got closer, they could see it was a building.

'Oh goody!' Princess Peach clapped her hands. 'It's someone's home! We can ask them where we are and how far away we are from the Mushroom Kingdom!'

'I'm not so sure about that.'

'Mario, why are you always so pessimistic? You always think the worst of people.'

'That's because they've usually kidnapped you and I have to fight them to get you back.'

'Hmph.' Peach folded her arms. 'You think I can't look after myself, don't you?'

Mario opened his mouth to say 'Yes, of course I do', but he shut it again. On this journey, he'd seen a different side of the Princess. He'd always been the one rescuing her, but he'd never taken the chance to get to know her properly. He didn't know what she could do when she wasn't ruling her kingdom. And the Toads loved her, didn't they? Had he really got the chance to know her?

'I'm sorry' he said to Peach. 'I thought you couldn't look after yourself, but you've got us out of every sticky situation so far on this trip.'

Peach blushed. 'Not on purpose.'

'It still counts! You've done more than I have to keep us going. I'm sorry if I made you feel useless. Forgive me?'

Peach nodded graciously. 'Of course I do.'

As they'd been talking, they'd drawn nearer to the building. Now they could see that it was an old mansion, tucked away here among the trees. The mansion itself had seen better days. Paint was peeling off the walls, the windows had mostly been broken and smashed in, and the roof was sagging like it couldn't stand up under its own weight any more. The trees around it were dead and broken, and the fence that surrounded the property was crumbling to bits.

Mario touched the gate to enter, and the creak of the hinges reverberated around the forests. He cringed. Every nasty out there would know they were here now.

'Do we go in?' asked Peach.

'I don't think we've got any choice', Mario replied.

Luigi was getting worried. It had been a couple of days now, and he was running out of books. Peach's bookcase had been stacked full of novels, but stuck in a room with nothing else to do, Luigi had just devoured them. At first, he'd picked one up because he was so bored and there was nothing else to do. Then, he started finding them hilarious, wiping the tears from his eyes as he howled like a hyena at them. Then, he realised he was actually getting into the books. He cared if the heroes of the story got together at the end. He cried real tears when the stories had tragic endings. He was invested.

But now, the choice available to him was looking rather threadbare. Only a few books were left. He picked one up off the shelf. He wasn't sure if Mario wasn't ever coming back, but he tried to ignore that thought. Nothing had happened to him. He was Mario. He was always ok.

To silence that nagging thought, Luigi opened the book and began to read.

* * *

The mansion creaked and groaned as they stepped onto the porch. With some trepidation, Mario knocked on the door. The knocks echoed around them.

'I don't like this' murmured Peach.

'Me neither.'

There was no answer. Mario knocked again. 'Hello?' he called through the letter slot. 'Is anyone home?'

There was still no answer. He looked back at Princess Peach.

'Try the door' she said.

Mario turned back and turned the handle. To his surprise, it opened easily. The door pulled out of his hand, and opened on its own. The mansion lay behind it, gloomy and foreboding. They could see a few feet of mouldy old carpet, and then nothing

'Do we have to go inside?' Peach asked. She was looking over Mario's shoulder, nose wrinkled in disgust. 'When was the last time this house was cleaned?'

'Some dust bunnies would be the least of our worries' said Mario, darkly. He stepped forward into the mansion, and Peach followed suit. As they were both over the threshold, the door slammed shut behind them. They both jumped in shock.

'ARGH!'

'Well, that was rude.' Peach bristled.

'Well, we're here now. There must be somebody here. Let's go looking.'

'Should we split up? Cover more ground?'

Mario looked around him. 'I wouldn't risk it. I think we'd never find each other again.'

They moved forward, and almost stumbled across a small table. It held a single candle in a candle holder, and a box of matches.

'How useful!' cried Peach.

'Someone was expecting us to be here' said Mario, lighting the candle. 'We'd better watch our backs.'

They carefully walked around the ground floor, checking every room as they went. The rooms were all full of dusty old furniture, threadbare curtains and more mouldy carpets, but there wasn't another soul to be seen.

'Maybe the house is just abandoned' said Peach brightly. 'That's why nobody's here.'

'Oh, someone's here all right. Stick close to me Princess, I don't like this one bit.'

They finished the ground floor, and went up the rickety old stairs to the next level. They continued their search, but to no avail. There just wasn't another soul to be seen anywhere.

'Should we call out to them? Maybe they're hiding.' Peach, Mario thought, was determined to think positive about this experience. Or any experience. He'd never seen her as much as frown until they embarked on their mission to get back home.

'We'd best not' he said. 'There may be a friend hiding, but there's also some bad guys waiting for us, too. Better not tell them where we are just yet.'

They searched the second floor and found no one, so they went up again. The mansion felt as though it went on forever. Room after empty room. Had anyone ever really lived here?

'What was that?' Mario swung round, nearly burning Peach with the candle.

'What?'

'I heard something...'

Mario trailed off. He was sure he'd heard giggling.

They carried on again. He heard it again, a faint sound of laughter...

He swung round again, but there was nothing there but Princess Peach.

'Are you sure you're not imaging it?' she asked.

'Maybe I am.' The mansion was getting to him. Focus! He told himself. He had to keep it together for Luigi's sake.

They continued on until Mario opened the door on what appeared to be an enormous ballroom. Peach ran past him and twirled around on the grimy dance floor. 'Look at it Mario!' she called to him. 'Look how beautiful it must have been! Oh, I should have one built in my home. Maybe I'll put it where the throne room is now. Bowser's made a mess of it anyway. Oh, wouldn't it be wonderful?' She continued twirling, her eyes closed, imagining it.

Mario stepped inside. He didn't notice the door close behind him.

Peach ran over, grabbed his hands, and pulled him around with her. 'Isn't it pretty? Even now, it's beautiful. What a shame no one lives here!'

As they spun round, Mario heard it again. That giggling! Who was it?

'Show yourself!' he yelled, breaking away from Peach and stumbling as he regained his balance. 'Stop hiding like cowards!'

The giggling continued. Mario looked around, wildly. They had to be here, somewhere ...

The walls of the dilapidated old ball room were lined with floor to ceiling mirrors. As Mario turned and looked around, he saw things flit in and out of them.

'Princess, look!' He pointed as something else fled out of sight.

'What is it?' Peach looked scared now, all thoughts of ball rooms now gone from her head.

Mario shook his head. 'I can't get a good look at them.'

The giggling got louder, and the figures in the mirrors grew faster and faster. They were surrounded now, at any minute something would jump out and attack them, he knew it.

Peach screamed. Mario looked where one gloved hand was pointing, trembling as it did so. In the mirror that lay right in front of them, a Boo was poised. The ghost was leering at them, towering behind them. It's jaws were open, revealing rows of pointy teeth. It liked it's ghostly lips.

Mario spun round to see the Boo floating right behind them. It shrunk down, embarrassed to be seen, and covered its eyes with its ghostly arms.

'Ah, I see you've met one of my friends.'

Chapter 17 – A New Villain, Again

The door opened at the end of the room, and Wario walked in. He sauntered across the dance floor as if he owned the place. Perhaps he did. Mario supposed it wouldn't be surprising for Wario to keep a house like this, just to play tricks on people.

He came up to them, and patted the Boo on the head. Well, he pretended to. He stopped his hand at where it's head should be, since if he tried to actually touch it his hand would go straight through it.

'They're delightful aren't they?' he grinned, revealing his own pointy teeth.

'Delightful? They're terrifying!' said Peach, still cowering in fear.

'Oh, nonsense. They're dears, really. They wouldn't hurt you.' He smiled at them. 'How are you enjoying your trip?'

Mario scowled at him.

'That bad, huh? You know, you're being very ungrateful. What a fantastic time you're having! Look at all the things you've seen! Isn't it neat? I'm rather jealous of you both.'

'It's your fault we're in this mess' Mario snarled. If he took one wrong step, just one …

'You have a nerve, Wario.' Princess Peach drew herself up to her full height again.]When we reclaim the Mushroom Kingdom, I'll remember this. Mark my words.'

'Oh you will, will you? I don't doubt it. Who wants to spend all her time locked up in her tower? Not you. Better that loser Luigi does it, eh?'

'Don't you talk about Luigi like that!' yelled Mario. Princess Peach grimaced.

'Your attitude is appalling' she told Wario.

'Oh sure, of course. I make sure to keep it that way. Well, anyway, I just wanted to pop in and say goodbye to you both before I go.'

'Where are you going?' asked Peach, panicked.

'Well, to your wedding, of course! Or what Bowser thinks is your wedding, anyway. When do you think Bowser will realise Luigi isn't you, Princess? I'm betting on about five years down the line. Won't Luigi's face be a picture?'

As Mario and Peach looked at him aghast, he turned to leave. 'Oh, you won't be leaving her, obviously. I can't have you both ruining things. Where would be the fun in that? Goodbye! It's been horrible knowing you!' He walked out the door.

The giggling started again.

Chapter 18 – Diplomatic Relations

Mario and Peach huddled together as the giggling reached a fever pitch in the abandoned ball room. The shadows began to move again the mirrors. Before long, they were surrounded by Boos. In a group, they were no longer shy, and were brazenly closing in on the heroic pair.

'Mario, what are we going to do?'

'I can't think of anything! They're too brave now, we can't stop them!' Mario panicked. This had never happened to him before. What was he going to do now?

The Boos drew in closer. The leader bared his teeth.

It was all over. Bowser was going to take over the Mushroom Kingdom. They wouldn't be able to save Luigi.

Princess Peach broke away from Mario and stepped forward, clearing her throat.

'Ahem.'

the Boos stopped, taken aback by her actions.

"I don't know if you know me, but I'm Princess Peach' she declared. 'I'm very pleased to meet you.'

The Boos looked at each other, confused.

'I feel like we've got off on the wrong foot' she continued. 'We all live in the Mushroom Kingdom, so I feel like we should get to know each other better. You, sir, what's your name?' she asked the leader.

'Er...' the lead Boo stumbled, having clearly no need to speak normally. 'I don't know. I'm a Boo. Everyone's a Boo. We're all Boos.'

'Well' said Peach, not missing a step, 'I'm very pleased to meet you, Boos. Now, we do need your help.'

'You do?' The lead Boo was clearly mystified, but while he was confused none of the Boos were trying to eat them. Peach looked back at Mario, who grinned and gave her a thumbs up.

'Yes, we do. We need to get back to my castle, and quite quickly. There's a rather unsavoury character who's going to do horrible things if we don't stop him. My friend is captured, and we need to save him.'

The Boos muttered amongst themselves. After a moment, the lead Boo asked, 'What will happen if you don't get there?'

'Well, Bowser will take over the Mushroom Kingdom. I don't know what he'd do with your mansion here, but I can't imagine it's anything good.'

There was more muttering, along with the odd cry of 'But I LIKE living here!' and 'But where would we go?' After another moment, the lead Boo turned round again.

'We have decided' he said.

'Oh, excellent! What have you decided?' Peach asked.

'We'll help you' he said. 'We like living here, and we don't like the sound of this Bowser guy'

'Oh, thank you so much! We need to get back as soon as we can. Can you help us?'

'Of course, follow me.' The lead Boo turned towards the door, and Mario and Peach followed.

Chapter 19 – The Awful Truth

'He's doing WHAT?'

The Koopa assistant sighed. 'He's marrying you.'

'But... what... I'm not Princess Peach!!'

'We know that. Everyone in the castle knows that. But he doesn't.'

Luigi fidgeted as another Koopa bustled around him with a measuring tape. 'Why don't you stop him?!'

'Have you tried stopping Bowser?' the Koopa asked.

'Yes. Many times. And it's worked' said Luigi, pointedly. 'Look, what's going on here? I'm not going along with this. Enough is enough!'

'What do you think will happen if he finds out you're not the Princess?' the Koopa assistant asked. 'What do you think he'll do to you?'

Luigi sagged. 'Good point.'

'Stand up straight!' the seamstress Koopa shrilled.

'Look, it's not great for anyone here. No one's happy. But for now, can you please go along with it? We've finally got some of the Toads on our side, and they're helping out. You won't suffer as long as we all stick together.'

'I suppose. I hope you've got something good up your sleeve though.'

'We'll see.' The assistant left, leaving Luigi to be poked with pins by the seamstress.

'I've never seen such an ugly princess' it remarked.

Luigi sighed.

* * *

The Koopa assistant met up with Bowser, as he was undergoing his spa day. In what used to be Princess Peach's bathroom, he lay in the enormous Jacuzzi, bubbles up to his chin. He wore a green face mask and cucumber slices over each eye.

'Your Horribleness...' started the assistant.

'Shhhhh! I'm relaxing' said Bowser, sinking lower into the bubbles.

The assistant wondered what the face mask was in aid of. It wasn't going to make him prettier, that was for sure.

'I'm sorry, Your Horribleness, but it's very important. It's good news' he added, hopefully.

Bowser cocked an ear at that.

'Is it? Tell me!'

'Well, I was speaking to our source, and he says that Mario is no more! The last time he saw him was in a haunted mansion, being ganged up on by a bunch of Boos.'

'No one can come out of that in one piece' Bowser remarked. 'How wonderful! Now nothing can ruin my wedding day!'

The assistant coughed slightly.

'What? What's wrong?' Bowser said suddenly.

'What? Oh, nothing' the assistant lied, hurriedly. 'Lots to get done, you know. Shall I go and check on the preparations?'

'Yes, you do that. Everything must be perfect.' Bowser sunk down again into the warm water. 'Ah, this is the life.'

Oh Bowser, the assistant thought. If only you knew.

Chapter 20 – Where Is Mario?

The Boos took Mario and Princess Peach into the basement of the mansion. It was possible that it was gloomier than the rest of the house combined. The air was dank with rot, and mould grew on almost every surface. Princess Peach stepped very carefully across the concrete floor to avoid the many puddles that were spread around.

The Boos stopped, then spread apart so they could reveal their plan to them both. 'This should help. We've heard about you Mario, and we know you sometimes use these?'

Behind them, looking like nothing more than a beacon of hope, was a green pipe.

'That's fantastic!' he beamed. 'Do you know where it goes?'

'We're not sure' said the Boo, 'but we know most pipes lead to the Mushroom Kingdom, right? It's bound to get you closer to your destination.'

'Yes, yes, that's right!' he turned to Princess Peach, who clearly felt sceptical but was doing her best not to show it. 'Are you ready to go?'

'Yes, I think so.' She turned to the Boos. 'Goodbye, Boos! Thank you so much for your help! We'll never forget you!'

'Good luck!' said the lead Boo. 'We hope you get your home back.'

'Me too.' Mario helped her up onto the pipe. She looked down and held her nose. 'Goodbye!' she called out, then jumped down. Mario climbed up after her and followed suit.

They slid down the pipe for what felt like miles. They slid round twists and turns, getting faster and faster, until they landed in a deep underground cavern. Princess Peach floated daintily down to the ground, using her skirts as a parachute. Mario made a less graceful entrance, thudding to the ground and rolling over.

'Oof!' He stood back up and shook himself off. 'Ok Princess' he said, 'Are you ready to get going?'

'Of course!'

'Let's go then.' He took her hand and they raced through the caverns together.

* * *

Morning had broken, and somewhere in the distance could be heard trumpets blaring. Luigi woke up groggily.

Oh.

Oh no.

It was the day of the wedding.

There was a banging on the door.

'Wake up now, it's time to get ready!' It was the seamstress.

Luigi flopped back down into bed. The door swung open, and the seamstress bustled in, acres of tulle and silk in their arms.

'Up, now, up! Out of bed! It's a busy day, you know. Can't keep His Horribleness waiting, can we?'

Luigi groaned.

'Oh, don't be like that. I've done the best I could. With a dress this pretty, no one will get a look at your ugly face.'

* * *

Guests were lining up at the gates of Peach's castle, ready for entrance to the wedding. The guests were mostly Toads, and they were grumbling about having to be there. Bowser had threatened to flatten them if they didn't come, though, so here they were.

Minions led them in a few at a time, and sat them down in the courtyard. A large flower arch had been erected at one end, on a small stage for the bride and groom to stand on. The Toads sat down and waited expectantly. There were hushed whisperings around the crowd.

Where was Mario?

Wasn't he here a few days ago?

Why hadn't he saved the day yet?

Chapter 21 – Our Villains Meet

'Name?'

'Wario.'

'Second name?'

'You don't need it. My name is Wario. His Horribleness is expecting me.'

The minion looked up at him. 'Oh, of course. We'll escort you to him.'

'Of course.' The gates were opened, and another minion beckoned for Wario to follow him.

As they walked through the castle grounds, Wario reflected on what a wonderful wheeze this had all been. That idiot Bowser was easier to play than a kiddie's computer game. All it took were a few well worded suggestions whispered into his scaly ear, and he'd stormed up here to claim the place. He didn't know how Mario and Luigi were going to react, but that was all part of the fun. He trotted after the minion, a big grin on his face.

They found Bowser in the throne room, with his assistant trying to wrestle a bow tie on him.

'Your Horribleness, you need to hold still!'

'I don't want to wear this thing! It's itchy! GRAAAAAAH!'

'Don't you want to look presentable on your big day?' The assistant got the bow tie on finally, and hopped down off Bowser's shoulder. Bowser looked in a nearby mirror.

'Well, it does look good' he admitted, preening.

'You look like a real gentleman, sir.'

The minion cleared his throat. 'Ahem. Wario is here to see you, Your Horribleness.'

'Ah yes, send him in, send him in. You' he said, pointing at his assistant. 'You can go.'

'Yes sir' he said, and scuttled away.

'Wario, my friend, how are you?' He leaned down and shook Wario's hand. 'Isn't it a wonderful day?'

'The best' Wario agreed, thinking privately, for me it is, yes. You're going to get a big shock, Lizard Boy.

'I have you to thank for it all' said Bowser. 'Finally, my dreams are in reach!'

'I do hope that means that he deal is still on' said Wario, amiably.

'Oh, of course, of course. Once I'm married, this castle will be mine, so you can take control of Bowser Fortress. Why do you want it, anyway?'

'Oh, I have my reasons' said Wario. 'Of course, it's not mine until the deed is done. When is the wedding, Your Lizardness?'

Bowser looked at the clock. 'In an hour' he said, readjusting his bow tie. 'You know, I'm not sure about this thing. It is very itchy.'

'It does suit you though' said Wario.

'Ah, doesn't it though?' Bowser preened in the mirror again.

Chapter 22 - To The Rainbow Road

Mario and Princess Peach had been running for what felt like forever. They didn't dare slow the pace down, not even for a moment. The wedding grew closer and closer, and the longer they left it the more Luigi and the whole Mushroom Kingdom were in danger.

Just as they thought they couldn't run any more, they began to see a light at the end of the tunnel. 'Come on!' puffed Mario, 'We're nearly there. Just a little bit further ...'

Princess Peach was too out of breath to reply.

They reached the end, and found a small lift platform under a bright light. They both jumped onto it and panted as it took them up into the daylight again. Before long, they found themselves high up in the sky, the ground stretching away below them.

'Where are we now?' asked Mario, confused.

'The Rainbow Road! Look!'

Peach pointed, and Mario saw it. The Rainbow Road was, as the name suggested, a rainbow that stretched away into the distance. Sometimes citizens used the road to race on, but today it was full of just normal commuters putting along in their cars.

'This road leads right to my castle! We're nearly there, Mario!'

Fantastic news! Mario saw one flaw, though. 'Are we going to walk the entire thing? We don't have time.'

They looked around. Nearby were two racing buggies, abandoned by the side of the road. Peach jumped in one. 'Come on!'

Mario jumped into the other buggy. 'Isn't this stealing, Princess?'

'It's a royal emergency! I'll send them back to the rightful owners once we're done. We don't have any other choice.'

Mario could agree with that. They started their buggies, and began accelerating down the Rainbow Road. Princess Peach overtook him early, and began speeding away down the road. She honked her horn, and the other drivers swerved out of her way as she screeched past.

'Sorry! It's an emergency!' she called, as the other drivers shook their fists.

Mario struggled to keep up with her He finally crept up behind her as the road was making its way into the Mushroom Kingdom proper. 'Princess, slow down!' he yelled.

'No! We don't have time! And besides, I'm having too much fun!' Princess Peach beeped the horn again and pulled ahead. Mario put the foot down himself and tried to keep up.

Peach was giggling like mad as they made their way into the kingdom. She spun around with abandon, taking the road as if it were no more difficult than a stroll through the park.

'This is brilliant!' she cried out. 'Why don't we do this more often!'

As they carried on, they could see Peach's home coming up in the distance. They could see banners laid out on the walls, and confetti being fired into the sky. Faintly, they could hear the sound of trumpets.

'Oh no, the wedding's started' breathed Mario. How long did they have left? Had Bowser caught onto the ruse? Was Luigi ok?

Princess Peach had noticed it too. 'Oh no, he doesn't' she thundered, all trace of a good mood gone. 'He can't have my castle and he can't have Luigi!' She slowed down until she was aside Mario's buggy. 'Come on, we have to get in there.'

'How?' Mario looked down from the road. The place felt as though it were miles away.

'Trust me.' Peach held out her hand.

Mario, not without some trepidation, took it.

'Now jump!'

'What?' But it was too late. Princess Peach had pulled him out of his buggy and they were falling towards the ground, at rather an alarming rate.

'Princess, we're going too fast!' he yelled.

'I thought you trusted me?' replied Peach. As she said so, her skirts opened like a parachute, and their fall turned into a gentle glide. They were falling right into the castle courtyard.

Chapter 23 - A Plan Is Formed

There was a knock on the door again.

'Come in', Luigi sighed.

The Koopa assistant came in, and looked at Luigi.

'I have something to tell you', he said.

'Yes, I know I look ridiculous.' Luigi was decked out in a full wedding dress and veil. Every inch of him sparkled and glittered. The look was completed by an oversized bouquet of roses that he was to take with him when they went to the ceremony.

'No, no, not that. Well, yes, you do, but that's not your fault. Sit down, sit down.'

Luigi manoeuvred himself onto the bed. There was a lot of skirts going on in his outfit, and he wasn't sure what to do with them all.

'Here's the thing Luigi, I've not been straight with you', the assistant said. 'You know that note you got a few days ago?'

'Yes, I remember. How do you know about it?'

'I know about it because I'm the one who wrote it.'

Luigi looked at him blankly. Him? But he was one of Bowser's minions. He was always by his side. They'd never work against him, would they?

But then he remembered. The note said they wanted to go home. Of course! The minions didn't want to live here! They wanted to live in Bowser's fortress, where they'd always lived. Why would they fight to stay somewhere they don't belong?

'We thought we'd have an idea by now. We didn't think the wedding would even happen. Bowser's not very good plans. He can't normally remember what's he's meant to be doing the next day, never mind next week.' The assistant talked in a rush, like he'd never spoken about this before. Luigi supposed he hadn't. 'Here's the thing. I don't want to work with him. I don't want to be here. We want to get out. And get you out, obviously. But we don't have any ideas!' He shook his head sadly. 'We don't know what to do.'

Luigi thought hard for a moment.

Hang on.

'Could you hand me that book, please?' he asked. The Koopa picked up the book Luigi pointed at, and handed it to him. Luigi riffled through the pages.

'Aha!' He found the page he was looking for. He handed it to the assistant to read. 'How's that for a plan?'

The Koopa read thoughtfully for a moment. A grin spread out over his face. 'Yes. Yes, this could work!'

Chapter 24 - An Unusual Wedding

Wario watched in the audience as Bowser stood awkwardly at the altar. The 'bride' was running late, and he was clearly getting nervous. Bowser, nervous? He'd never thought he'd see the day.

He wondered if Luigi had made a run for it. Maybe he'd made some friends in the castle and they'd busted him out. He had no idea how, as security was so tight. Nothing could get in or out, as far as he could see. They'd been very clear about that.

If Luigi had escaped, it would be an awful shame. Everyone here would miss out on the awful spectacle of Bowser marrying the moustachioed plumber. Why, what would happen when he found out. Sparks would fly, no doubt.

Still, Luigi abandoning him was still chaotic enough for his tastes. Eventually, Bowser would have to give up waiting at the altar. How would he tell his would be subjects that sorry, but he wasn't going to rule over them after all?

Ah, no, scratch that. If they didn't get hitched, he'd never get his mitts on Bowser's fortress. No, Luigi had better turn up. He'd just better.

Just as he was getting worried that the plumber wasn't going to turn up after all, the organ at the back of the courtyard began to belt out the wedding march. Everyone turned to look, except Bowser, who kept looking in the opposite direction. Wario supposed that he didn't want to ruin the surprise.

Oh, if only he knew.

Everyone in the audience spotted straight away that it wasn't Princess Peach in the wedding dress. There were many hushed whispers around the courtyard, but nobody said anything. Good, thought Wario. He wanted this moment to stretch out for as long as possible.

Luigi walked nervously up the aisle. If he saw Wario, he didn't show that he recognised him. He moved forward, eyes front and centre. It was as if he had resigned himself to his fate.

He reached the stage, and Bowser turned round. Wario held his breath. Was this it? Was Bowser going to see who his blushing bride really was? The whole audience held their breath with him.

Bowser grinned his horrible, toothy grin, and held out a meaty claw. Grimacing, Luigi took it.

Wario had to do everything in his power not to start cackling with glee. He didn't notice! He couldn't tell his 'Princess Peach' was Luigi in a dress! This was better than he could have ever imagined!

With Luigi up on the stage, the reverend officiating the ceremony began his opening spiel. The whole audience watched with bated breath to see what would happen next. What had started as a sad, miserable day for the Mushroom Kingdom had suddenly turned hopeful, and full of surprises. What would happen next?

Chapter 25 - Bowser Doesn't Get It

The officiant reached the part Luigi had been waiting for. He stood stock still next to Bowser. He couldn't believe he had got this far. How had he not recognised him? The plan might even go off. This was insane. Everything was insane. How could this happen?

'If anyone knows of any lawful impediment, why these two people can't become Lizard and Wife, please speak now, or forever hold your peace.'

There was a hushed silence.

Somewhere in the back, a voice yelled, 'BECAUSE SHE'S NOT PRINCESS PEACH!'

The crowd gasped. Why did they gasp? They already knew. In any case, Luigi tore his veil off.

'That's right!' he cried, to screams and whoops from the Toads in the audience. 'It's me, Luigi!'

Bowser looked at him in utter horror.

'What are you doing?' he asked.

'I'm showing you who I really am! Luckily for her, the Princess is very far away and safe from your evil clutches!'

The officiant also looked horrified. 'You're not Princess Peach?' he asked, peering through his thick glasses.

'No, I'm not. Isn't it obvious?' Luigi was confused. 'Can't you tell?'

Bowser looked heartbroken now. For an awful moment, Luigi thought he might cry. 'But... why would you lie to me, Princess?'

Luigi was stunned into silence. So was the audience.

'...I'm not lying to you. I'm Luigi.'

'Princess, stop fighting it' said Bowser, with tears in his eyes. 'We're meant to be together.' He looked around at the audience below him. 'The wedding goes on as planned!'

He pulled Luigi closer to him. 'You'll see, we're meant to be together. Stop fighting it, Princess. You'll love it.'

Uh oh.

Chapter 26 - Saving The Day

The officiant droned on while Luigi panicked. He looked round to see the Koopa assistant in the back, also panicking. What were they going to do? The plan had failed! Why had it failed?

Luigi had been reading *Koopas In Love* before the assistant had come to him, and it was that book that gave him the inspiration for the escape plan. The lady Koopa was about to marry the awful bounder Koopa, but then the Koopa hero had run into the church, and when the group were asked if they couldn't be married, he'd yelled out 'BECAUSE SHE'S IN LOVE WITH ME!' In the book, the lady Koopa had run away with the hero, and they'd lived happily ever after. The book had lied to him.

Just as he thought there was no way out, he could hear renewed mutterings coming from the audience. He didn't dare turn around again, as Bowser had a firm grip on him.

The mutterings became full on gasps and cheers from the crowd. The officiant ignored them all and kept on burbling away. Bowser turned round to face them, taking Luigi with him.

'KEEP QUIET!' he roared. For the first time in his life, his roars went utterly ignored. Many were pointing up into the sky now, and jumping up and down in their chairs.

'Look! He's here! He's finally here!'

Luigi looked up, too. Up in the sky, they were very distant, but he recognised that red hat... it was Mario! It had to be! And... was that Princess Peach? She'd returned safely with him!

Luigi could barely stop himself from jumping up and down in glee. It was all going to be ok after all!

The pair floated down, down, down, until they dropped right in front of the stage. They both gawped at the scene around them.

A voice in the crowd yelled 'Mario! YOU WERE MEANT TO BE BOO CHOW!' It was Wario, shaking his fist and going red with fury. Mario and Peach ignored him. Princess Peach walked up to Bowser, crossed her arms, and said 'What on EARTH do you think you are doing? Unhand Luigi at once!'

'Wha... Princess... but...' Bowser looked at Luigi, then at Princess Peach, then back to Luigi again. 'But...' His mind had clearly short circuited.

Mario leapt forward and pulled Luigi from Bowser's unresisting grip.

'Are you ok Luigi? You're not hurt, are you?'

'I'm fine, I'm fine. Only my pride' Luigi shrugged.

Bowser's face was contorting, as he struggled to fit the pieces together. 'You... you're Princess Peach, aren't you?' he said to Peach.

'Yes, obviously. Now, take your minions and get OUT of my castle. Never show your face here again, and don't you dare hassle the inhabitants of the Mushroom Kingdom!' Any sensible creature would have cowered under Peach's tone. However, Bowser wasn't sensible.

'I don't think so, Princess. You're coming with me.' He reached out that meaty claw to grab the Princess, but she stepped back deftly out of his reach. He roared his disapproval.

'YOU ARE MINE!' he yelled in her face. Princess Peach's hair blew back, but she didn't even flinch.

'I don't think so' she said. 'I don't belong to anyone.'

Mario, Luigi and Peach were all aware of a scurrying behind them. Suddenly, a swarm of minion were streaming around them, but they weren't touching them. Instead, they were heading for Bowser. They picked him up and held him on his back. He flailed, roared, and kicked out, but they held him tight.

'We are going home, Your Horribleness' said the assistant Koopa. 'You need to learn where you belong.'

The minions cheered as they carried out of the main gates and out of sight. The Toads cheered along with them. As he was carried away, they could just hear Bowser yell, 'I'll get you for this, Mario!'

Mario shrugged. 'I've heard it before.'

Chapter 27 - All's Well

The cleanup operation was underway. Mario, Peach, and Luigi, who was finally back in his own clothes, were watching the work from a balcony.

'Where did Wario go? Princess Peach asked them. 'He was gone before Bowser was carried off.'

'He's probably fled to wherever he calls home, to think up another awful plan. He's a shady one, but I don't think we have to worry about him any time soon.' Mario peered over the balcony. 'The Toads are working quickly, aren't they?'

'They're just happy that Bowser got kicked out' said Luigi. He had already told the pair about his time impersonating Peach. 'Who knew they'd prefer Bowser's run down old castle to your place, Princess?'

'They're all very odd creatures', said Peach.

'You can say that again' said Mario. 'So, what now?'

'Well, I think we go see how the new ball room's coming along, don't you?' Peach took a brother on each arm. After that, I think we should go have some cake. I think we deserve it, don't you?'

Mario and Luigi both nodded. They definitely deserved a nice slice of cake after the last few days.

They all turned around, and went back inside.

Chapter 28 - Or Is It?

Wario panted his way up the steps, and burst his way through the doors. Creatures fled from his path as he wound his way up to Bowser's throne room.

Stupid Mario! He was supposed to be eaten by Boos! No one got away from the Boos! How had he done it? Wario seethed. Mario was always one step ahead, and it wasn't fair! He was meant to get this castle! Bowser should have given it to him!

No matter. If he couldn't have the fortress given to him, he'd take it by force.

He'd slipped out of the ceremony as the others had fought, and began running his way here. He knew Bowser would make his way back, and he needed to beat him. Had to. I he didn't, it would all be over.

He reached the throne room. He opened the door... and the room was empty. The amount of dust on the floor told him it had been a while since anyone had entered.

Perfect.

He walked outside to a balcony, whipped out a homemade crown, and plonked it on his head. He called out to the confused minions below him.

'BEHOLD! IT IS I, KING WARIO! BOW BEFORE ME!'

As the minions bowed, he cackled manically.

Made in the USA
San Bernardino, CA
15 March 2017